THE ALLAGASH

By

KENN BROOKS

TABLE OF CONTENTS

Roberta Scruggs photo

Kenn Brooks, left, and Ray Reitze move in for a closer look at an osprey's nest high above Musquacook Stream.

RAYMOND REITZE

The Allagash was near and dear to Ray; the Company he kept was even better.

Roberta Scruggs photo

Maine guide Ray Reitze, foreground, has made about 50 trips down the Allagash, while his brother-in-law, Kenn Brooks, has made two.

wholesome. Beans, rice, spaghetti, muffins, biscuits – even homemade doughnuts. Actually quite inventive when you consider it had to last four people a week with no chance to refresh the cooler's ice.

But I dreamed of a medium-rare cheeseburger with fries and the largest glass of milk I could lift. And just one crisp, juicy apple.

We amused ourselves by wondering if a confirmed nature-lover like Ray would mind if a Burger King – tastefully designed, of course – were erected nearby with a paddle-through. And I kept thinking of those cartoons where shipwrecked companions begin to resemble roast turkeys to one another.

With the sun high and hot, we stopped at Cunliffe Island and hung everything out to dry, so the camp looked like a town after a tornado.

We also had our one and only chance to bathe and it took more courage than I expected to walk into that brown river water. The bugs finally drove me under, but the cold water forced me right back to the surface. After a few quick dips, I felt great – but I'm really glad I didn't know until later about the giant bullfrog living in that little cove.

I tried to manage minor cleanups every day, even though a look into the mirror after the first full day was quite discouraging. It revealed a bright red gash across my forehead – I have no idea how I got it – that made me look like one of the Manson followers.

My hair was so plastered down with bug spray and rain that no matter how I combed it I looked exactly like Hitler – if Hitler had lived to be 90.

But Wednesday's sun not only dried our gear, it almost made us giddy. We joked and talked until nearly dusk, when I left for one last trip to the outhouse, aptly nicknamed the "hole of hell."

I was about 10 yards away when I heard a tremendous crashing ahead. I looked up to see a moose about 30 or 40 yards away and running like a race horse straight at me.

I ran, or more precisely, jumped like a jackrabbit to the right side of the outhouse, getting in just as the moose went by on the left.

I couldn't help giggling as I latched the hook and eye on the door. It seemed pathetically inadequate to stop the huge creature. But I locked it just the same.

Then I stood on the commode and looked through the wire window. The moose, which had a calf with her, stopped about 15 yards away, between me and the camp.

"Guys, there's a moose coming," I yelled.

No reply, just a flurry of move

Allagash Wilderness Waterway

Staff art by Pete Gorski

Kenn's hat even at top speed. I retreated into the hood of my raincoat and sneered as they snubbed their noses on its rubber surface.

I have been known to carefully free moths and rescue overturned beetles, but my attitude became, "Get them before they get you." When a flattened bug of unknown origin fell out of my jeans, my only thought was, "Hah! You'll never bite again."

In my loathing, I was only following in the footsteps of travelers

pressure on the waterway doubled as groups frantically tried to finish up. There was fierce competition for campsites and a traffic jam of sorts at Allagash Falls.

Several groups portaged while we did and nearly every man I talked to said wistfully he wished his wife had come but she was afraid of the bugs, hated canoes, didn't like camping or whatever. The men outnumbered the women about 10-1. It struck me as kind of sad.

RAY AND NANCY IN FRONT OF THEIR HOGEN CABIN

DEDICATION

I dedicate this series of Allagash River Trips to my Brother-in-Law and Guide Raymond E. Reitze, Jr. for taking me on four trips and teaching me about the Allagash Area and the lore of the early loggers in the area. The stories will tell you much of it.

And to his Wife, my sister Nancy (Brooks) Reitze, as she helped with the stories, was on three of my trips and on a lot with Ray and friends and clients.

I love you much and love you dearly.

Thanks,

Brother Kenn

The Allagash Wilderness Waterway

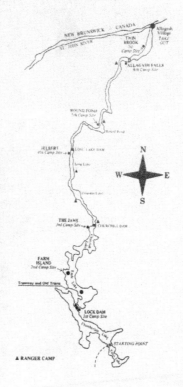

Canoe the Allagash River with Ray

RAY'S GUIDE SERVICE
RAY REITZE, JR.
Registered Maine Guide
Member Maine Professional Guides Association

The Allagash River Canoe Trip is a 98-mile trip from Chamberlain Lake to Allagash Village. This trip is an eight day vacation full of adventure, from wildlife to the beautiful skies and setting sun!

11

My Brother-in-Law Raymond E. Reitze, Jr. better known as Ray Reitze or just Ray, a Master Maine Guide, a builder of Cedar-Strip Canoe's, Snowshoes, and a Basket Weaver. Sister Nancy specializes in Medical Herbs. They both have lectured at Unity College, L.L. Bean Shows, and the Audubon and The Maine Sportsmen Shows in Augusta. Ray has also studied Indians of Maine, New York and the Western States and has become quite a philosopher.

I wanted to go on an Allagash trip in the worst way. I had been learning and helping Ray make canoes for upcoming trips. Ray's girls and their cousins also had been wanting to go on one of Ray's trips. So, Ray put together a summer family trip from Churchill Dam to Allagash Village where the waterway flows into the

St. John River to Allagash Village above Fort Kent.

Ray and Nancy's daughters Lenore and April, their nephews Jarred Reitze and Danny Lewia and I went on this trip together. Before we left, he added two helicopter pilots.

The trip from Canaan to the waterway is a 6-hour drive to put in, down the waterway, and back to Canaan can be made in seven days. Ten days will give you more time for sightseeing and taking off a day for rain (a rainy-day layover). Nancy could not make this trip.

This was my first trip into the North Maine Woods. We left Canaan and took a shortcut to the East side of Skowhegan, then on to Athens, Harmony, Guilford, Abbott Village, Monson, and into Greenville. This is the last stop for gas, ice, soda, and snacks.

Next, you go onto the Golden Road, now it's all dirt roads. Ten miles up the Lilly Bay to the Telos Road, another ten miles to the Telos Check Point into the North Maine Woods.

You must pay so much a person per day for the time you will be there. Then it's a long way to the road into Indian stream and continue by another long way into Churchill Dam.

Once there you unload your gear, and the rangers take it to an old bridge site below Chase Rapids, something they do because too many people have turned over in the rapids and lost everything. The rapids are right after the dam. Ray asked me about my experience with whitewater and if I knew how to read the water, to choose the path between the rocks. Answer: not experienced in picking the best route, but enough to be able to follow you and long as I'm not too many turns behind you.

Ray said, "O, K., Kenn, you and Jared follow April and me, then the pilots and Danny and Lenore will bring up the rear." We all made it safely and stopped to pick up the gear that the rangers had dropped off for us. As we were loading things into the canoes, Ray said, "Kenn, there's no way I'm going to carry your two sixpacks of Mt. Dew."

Our first camp site was at Chisholm Brook, up on a hill overlooking Umsaskis Lake, I had gotten my boots wet, after making a campfire in a rock fire pit, I put my boots on the top of the rocks to dry. Ray had gone down to get water for cooking and the novice that I was, I put too much wood on the fire. I "cooked my boots" and burnt a hole in the tarp overhead.

The wind comes up with the sun and goes down with the sun. Ray's strategy is to get up early the next morning and leave early to get ahead of everyone else and the wind, work our way down river to have your pick of the campsites. When you get to that campsite, you set up tents, put the tarp over the picnic table, and get firewood.

Then, without all the gear in the canoe you can go on looking for Moose or other wildlife, Eagles, Osprey, Ducks, or Geese that are around as well. Fishing is only great on the early spring trip.

Our next camp site was Sam's on Long Lake. Ray said he remembers, "One of the pilots fooling with Jarred, holding him up by his feet and ducking his head under water."

One morning, Jared said, "He was hungry, and he could eat anything." Ray had quite a bit of pancake batter left over, so he made a pan-sized pancake about two inches thick for Jarred and he could not get it all down.

I had a disposable camera designed to take photos underwater and had not found a good subject to try it on. We were swimming so I tried it on Ray's big toe.

The photos are those that show how canoes are made and the pictures of the two Indian girls were put on my canoe. The following photo show our arrival at Churchill Dam on the road built on top of the dam. Danny Lewia looking at the river.

On the next morning out, we had been through a shower and had wet clothes. We stopped on at Cunliffe Island on Long Lake for lunch and the wind was blowing right at us with large white caps on the lake. Ray wanted to cross the lake to the left side to go down on the left side to the next campsite. Ray also said the wind would go down in a couple of hours. We then hung clothes to dry on the bushes and tree limbs to dry in the sun.

19

In came a swarm of black flies, out came the head nets and gloves to cover our heads and hands. Ray still tried to take a nap to no avail. I sat on a large rock, the black flies would land on my blue denim dungarees, I would slap them killing 10 to 20 at a time, over and over again, for some time.

That experience with the black flies taught me well, I never went on another trip without a net. But over the next half dozen trips I never needed it again. But like many things if you need it, you want to have it available.

While we were doing this, we heard a low flying jet coming, looked up to see the pilot and his emblems on his helmet, and he was gone in a flash. We heard another one coming, never saw it only to realize that the first one was by us before we had looked up to see the second one.

21

They were doing low-level flying drills using their new radar like bats to keep them from flying into things.

All I could think of was how the African Natives of the South Pacific when they looked up to see their very first airplanes, especially when they were shooting at each other.

When the wind died down, clothes dried, off we went across the lake and down the river.

As we entered Pelletier's Dead Water, I saw a fishing pole in about seven feet of clear water. The current carried us away from it. We paddled back upstream and floated back down three times, looking for it. It looked nice and new, but we could not find it again. I knew I could have dived down from shore and retrieved it.

As you approach Allagash Falls there are signs telling you to stay right and take out for the half-mile portage. There are three campsites about halfway across, they are usually taken. It's an easy half day trip to Allagash Village. Ray likes to get to the falls just before noon, do all the lugging of the gear before lunch and then go looking at the two faces that can be seen in the rocks with a short walk. Only once was I there when the water was too high after rains, and you could not see them. Then move down to Big Rock campsite on the right-hand side.

The next morning, a half day out, we loaded up the truck and went to lunch at the restaurant after days on the water and eating our own cooking. This makes for an early start for the trip home. We stopped at the Lumberman's Museum in Patten on the way home as Ray was the only one who had been there before.

24

Picture #1 is April Reitze looking at the old Lombard.

Picture #2 is Danny Lewia setting up camp.

Picture #3 is the face of the Old Man in Allagash Falls.

Picture #4 is another out crop at the Falls.

Picture #5 is looking back at Allagash Falls as we leave.

Picture #6 is the Lumberman's Museum in Patten.

THE VERMONT BROTHERS TRIP TO ALLAGASH LAKE (See Map 55 of the Maine Atlas and Gazetteer by De Lorme)

RICHARD AND PETER RODEN

Raymond and Nancy Reitze attended the Vermont Sportsman Show to get more canoe customers. They took a sample canoe with them, and Ray ended up trading it for a fly rod. Ray said, "I knew I could build another canoe and it was the only way I would ever get that expensive pole."

He also met Peter Roden and discussed building him a canoe and doing a trip when he and his brother Dick came to take delivery. Ray wanted to add the Allagash Lake Trip to his list of trips, and this would be his first trip to the lake. We would use Allagash Stream that flows into and out of the lake.

To learn the building process, I had to help make the canoe and was invited to be Ray's" boat mate" on the trip with them.

On the appointed weekend I was there waiting at Ray's when in rolled a green dump truck. We were wondering who it could be when I noticed the Vermont license plate.

Ray said, "All the way from Vermont in a dump truck." And we had a good laugh.

After the introductions were done, we found out that they each had left cars at home for their wives. When the new canoe was inspected, loaded, and fastened down, we left with them following Ray's Ford Bronco.

The usual track to Skowhegan, Athens, Harmony, Guilford, Abbott Village, Monson, and to Greenville. Last stop for gas, ice, drinks, and snacks. Then it was off to the Golden Road, all dirt roads the rest of the way, ten miles to the Telos Road, another ten miles or more to Telos Creek Point into the North Maine Woods. Pay so much a person per day for the use of the roads for the time you will be there. Then we continued onto Cyr Road, crossing St. John's Bridge onto Russell Stream Road and down to the Narrow Pond Road.

We were looking for a good spot where the Narrow Brook flows into

Allagash Stream coming from Allagash Pond. The signpost was gone, Ray decided to leave Dick and Pete at the gravel pit, while he and I went several more miles to the intersection with the Saint Aurelie Road and to make sure we had found the proper place to leave the trucks for their transport and the right place to start the canoe trip. We set up our night camp in that small gravel pit which had been used to get material for the road maintenance. We had a nice time exchanging stories and getting to know each other better. Ray has a way of presenting his lessons without upsetting the students, so to speak.

Breakfast out of the way, things packed up, and everything was lugged across the road. Then the canoes were put into the stream and loaded up. We had to walk the canoes a way, to get them into deeper water before we could get in.

We stopped along the way for sandwiches and got to Allagash Lake early afternoon. We looked over Ledge Point and Sandy Point Campsites and decided on the latter. Set up camp, found wood, started a fire, and got fishing gear ready for the next day.

The next morning after chow we went fishing for the day, the Vermonters got three fish and we went over and explored the island and the "Ice Cave" and enjoyed lunch (sandwiches) then fished on our way back to camp. Then moved

camp to the outlet site and set up
camp again and enjoyed another
campfire. The fishing the next
morning didn't improve. So, we
decided to pull up camp and take
Allagash Stream down to Little
Round Pond and set up at Little
Allagash Falls. Here the fishing was
good, and we filled the skillet for
supper, a very nice treat. The Ranger
came by to warn us about the falls
which had a five-foot drop into logs
hung up on large rocks. He told us
how to portage around it.

The next day, with the portage done,
we left in very good spirits as the trip
was going well, we were all having
fun. Then in one spot we came

around a turn and looking ahead we could see that the water dropped out of eyesight, and just before that it looked like the water split on two sides of a small island. We put ashore on the island to scout the waterway ahead. The left side was narrow and shallow, the right side looked just deep enough and just wide enough with a large ledge on the right side. There was a large rock on the left side, as the water flowed into a good size pool before the waters joined at the end of the island.

Being near noon and being out on land we decided to eat lunch. When we got ready to go Dick wanted to take his turn at the controls. They were on our right side, so they were going to go ahead around the island. When they pushed off the current grabbed their canoe, and they started down backwards. They could have made it that way and turned around in the pool beyond the ledge. But Dick tried to turn it right then

and they went sideways. As I said, there was a large rock on the left and the ledge on the right, the canoe went up against them both, and the canoe turned over sideways and lodged there.

We rescued as much of the gear we could. We could not find one paddle, one life jacket, and Dick's brand new $500.00 fly pole in a metal case. We had to cut two poles with a dull axe, to use to pry the canoe free. This took us over two hours. At one point I took a photo of the canoe on its side. Half full of water about to break. The saving factor was that the rock and ledge held the canoe suspended with some water going under it. By the time we got the canoe pried out of the ledge, on the upstream side had shaved off a piece of the bow 2 inches deep and about 8 inches long. Ray had to

make a new bow piece out of a piece
of cedar, and duck taped it in place
for the rest of the trip. It was

months later before I showed the photo to Ray, as I wasn't sure he wanted to see the evidence that would produce publicity.

Next, we all walked in the 18 inches of water, back and forth trying to turn up the fly pole, to no avail. As we moved down stream in the canoes looking for the other two items, the paddle was spotted hung up in some bushes. All four of us never saw the life jacket again.

The next camp was on a beautiful beach at the end of Chamberland Lake. There was a couple already set up on one end, as we came in, I thought the man looked familiar. After we set up camp, I walked over to say hello and found out it was Mr. Cramer from Westbrook, Maine. We knew each other from the Cumberland County Republican Committee. He said they camped there for two weeks every summer, you had to boat everything across the lake, he wanted to make the trips over and back worthwhile.

The next morning, we went about halfway down Chamberland to the Tramway. We checked out the old Steam Plant and then ported all our stuff the ¾-mile along the tramway making several trips to Eagle Lake and the site of the two locomotives. One 90-ton and the other 100-ton, we looked them all over and walked along two old tracks looking at the remains of the log hauling cars. There are over 50 of them.

Then we reloaded the canoes and went down the left side of Eagle Lake by Farm Island and Hog Island to the Pumphandle Campsite. After camp was set up Ray took us up to the second ridge overlook, looking back from where we came.

The next morning down the rest of Eagle Lake, through Round Pond and down Churchill Lake to Churchill Dam, we loaded the trucks and went home in reverse of the way we came in. The only time I went home that way. It was the summer of 1989.

by Farm Island and Hog Island to the Pumphandle Campsite.   After camp was set up, Ray took us up

The following was taken from a Book, "A Treasury of the Maine Woods" by Edmund Ware Smith "A Downeast Quality Reprint".

THE BIRD WITH THE LONESOME VOICE

The common loon, Gavia Gimmer, not only defies classification, but has the vocal talent to laugh at it. As a personality, he is impervious, somber, amiable and given to clowning. As a creature, he is the size and roughly the shape of a small goose, and is composed of wings, feathers, webbed feet and bill. Add to this fact that the loon can fly and lay eggs, and you have the chief reasons why people call him a bird.

*There is evidence to the contrary.
The loon can swim a great deal
better than he can fly. Moreover, he
can swim better underwater than on
it. While submarining, he uses his
wings as a seal uses flippers. So, the
look seems to be a combination of
fish, fowl, and seal.*

*The one feature which distinguishes
the loon from all his contemporaries,
human or otherwise, is a voice which
in a single cry expresses the haunting
loneliness of the wild places of the
earth. Quite distinct from the eerie
laughter of this waterfowl's storm
call, its wilderness cry is far reaching
and sorrowful. But the loon is not
altogether tragic. He loves comedy
and play. By an exchange of calls
between hidden coves and lakes from
Maine to Labrador, he gathers
cronies to gossip sessions, communal
fishing expeditions, or for
rambunctious aquacades.*

*On sighting a school of minnows, the
loon dives with infinite grace, the*

long-pointed bill knifing the water, the body following in a smooth, otter-like disappearance. With filled air chambers, he can stay under water for about twenty minutes. Frequently, as if for a prank, one will come up with a loud splash beside your canoe. In split second he has sucked on a refill of air.

If laying eggs is proof of being a bird, the loon just barely makes the class. The female lays scarcely enough eggs to admit use of the plural – one or two olive-drab ovoid with brown specks. Unfortunately, loons have to go on land to build their nests, a compulsion which reduces of homemaking. The loon afoot makes a sorry showing. He can just barely walk; He and his mate resemble a crochety old couple with arthritis in their backs and chilblains in both feet.

So, their nest is built approximately two feet above high-water mark. The less hiking the better.

The egg, or eggs, hatch in about three weeks. The parents teach the young loon to swim and dive before anything else. It is a joy to observe the young one's training, his parents circling him, shrieking instructions, or showing him by example.

The young loons change from a brownish color to quickly black and white. But they usually gain full plumage in time for migration, which extends south to the Gulf of Mexico north to Labrador.

There is not much difficulty in finding a loon's nest in June or early July. If, while paddling your canoe close to shore, you get near a nest, the mother will come charging out, wailing, and shrieking. She will volplane on the lake surface for as much as a quarter of a mile, luring you from the nest. Follow her wake back to shore, look sharp, and you'll find the nest under overhanging alders of a cedar frond.

Loons, in groups of two to six, swim by our float on Mattagamon Lake, in Maine, several times each day in season. A white towel waving on a stick arouses their curiosity, and to investigate it they come so close we can see their black and white checked backs, the white ring on their necks, and even their eyes and bills.

We have learned to imitate many of their calls. But there is one we can't master-the wilderness call. This seems to be protected by the loon's primordial copyright, filed on some secret dead water up near the Arctic Circle.

Once on a still morning in March, we heard the call down in Florida on the Gulf Coast. Spring was coming, and that mysterious, poignant, heartbreaking voice told of the silent lakes of the north. Its ascending wail carried the symbol of distance and the meaning of wild places. It is the loneliest voice on earth."

TRIP NUMBER THREE Dates 6-21 to 6-30-1992

Maine Sunday Telegram article written by staff writer Roberta Scruggs Sunday July 12, 1992.

Subtitle: On the Allagash this 90mile Canoe trip is no walk on the beach. Roberta wanted to do a trip and story on the Allagash. Her canoe partner would be husband, George Krohne. Through friends she was referred to Guide Raymond Reitze. Ray asked me to be his partner in the front of the canoe. He tried to teach me the "Draw Stroke", but I had been in the back so many years that my instinct was to do something else.

Now her story was so good from her perspective that I'm going to use it and only once in a while adding in an anecdote of my own.

Roberta says, "Nothing comes easy on the Allagash. There are great highs and great lows and only the traveler himself knows if one is worth the other. And then only at the end."

The four of us began the six-hour drive to the river from Ray's Canaan home at daybreak Sunday June 21, pulling two of his beautiful handmade cedar strip canoes on a trailer.

Ray, 46, is not just an experienced Maine Guide, he's also a very enthusiastic one although it may take a while to discern the enthusiasm in his stolid manner. He's not a large man, but he's wiry, and strong enough to carry a cedar canoe alone across the half-mile portage at Allagash Falls.

At first, he seems tight-lipped and undemonstrative, but we grew to enjoy his wry laugh. One night while we talked in camp, he mentioned he once thought of being a jet pilot. We were dumbstruck. Ray, after all, insists on life in the slow lane. His knowledge and interest fit him perfectly for the 1800s.

But he just smiled, the corners of his mouth barely rising. "When I told my mother that," he said, "She just looked at me in the eye and said, Ray, you're toooooooooo Slooooooow."

We laughed so hard the picnic table shook.

Kenn is much more excitable than his brother-in-law. A man of 50 with powerful shoulders, he had greater canoeing skills than George and me, but suffered the same stiffness after paddling five or six hours a day. "By the third day, I was dying," he said later.

But Kenn, who makes his living in real estate, was fueled by the fervor of his love for wildlife. He greeted the appearance of each moose and deer with the enthusiasm some reserve for a long-lost Army buddy.

For my husband and me, this was a great adventure. George, a newspaper man turned adult education teacher, was worn down by a hard winter and, at 44, very much wanted a new challenge. As for me, an element of defiance increased my eagerness. With age 40 rushing toward me, I wanted to do something big, tough, and physical. I didn't intend to settle quietly into middle age.

Ray has made about 50 trips down the Allagash, while his brother-in-law, Kenn Brooks, has made two.

The adventure really began when we lined the canoes about a mile down Indian Pond Stream into Eagle Lake. Lining means holding onto ropes attached at the bow and stern and walking the canoe through shallow water like a large dog on a leash.

Then it was only a few miles to our campsite on Pillsbury Island, where Henry David Thoreau stayed on one of his trips to the North Maine Woods. The first taste of paddling illustrated clearly the need to work up to a 90-mile river trip.

I had not developed much stamina canoeing on placid ponds. Every few minutes, I wanted to change my paddle from one side of the canoe to the other to ease the pain. But Ray insisted we paddle on one side - otherwise steering minutes becomes a nightmare and energy is wasted.

And just to test our resolve a little more, it started raining Monday as we left camp. The kind of rain that makes people in nice, cozy offices say, "It's coming straight down."

It came down my arms, soaking my sleeves and straight down my rain gear into my inadequate Bean-clone boots.

It was a hard day, really the hardest of all. George and I seemed to be going different direction, my paddling was pitifully inefficient, and

my arms turned to lead.

Dubious about my ability, Ray tried to instruct me, while wondering if we could ever complete this trip in the allotted time.

He had brought along a motor and so we zoomed out to see two giant steam engines, once used for a logging tramway, but so long abandoned a small tree grew on one.

It was interesting, but the mosquitoes were so thick you could inhale them if you didn't breathe carefully. So, we moved on.

Then we stopped at the Pump Handle and climbed high enough to see the waterway for miles in either direction. The view was beautiful even in the relentless rain.

But the beauty evaporated for me when Ray began to think out loud about all the improvements needed in my technique. I started back down, getting angrier with every step. At the bottom, I decided I wasn't going to suffer in silence for seven days.

"I'm beginning to get the impression you think I'm a real drag on this trip," I burst out. "I never told you I was an expert paddler. I'm trying as hard as I can, and I think it's unrealistic to expect miracles the first day out. And I don't want to spend the whole week being pressured and badgered."

I laugh now to think of the shocked expression on Ray's face – as if some inanimate object had suddenly roared at him – but it wasn't funny at the time. He said he was sorry if I felt like that and if it seemed that way again to just hit him with a paddle. I said, don't worry I will.

Later, Kenn said maybe they just tried to tell us too much, too fast. And Ray told us it usually takes about three days for people to leave behind whatever emotional stress thy brought along for the ride.

In a way, though, the early blowup worked out well. We all abandoned a polite, but distant, relationship and began to be real with each other.

None of us is the compliant type. All four have somewhat thorny personalities, with a large streak of don't-tread-on-me stubbornness. Once we learned to give each other plenty of room, the anxiety level dropped all the way around.

TRAPPED IN THE RAPIDS

Since we were now talking, George and I told Ray we didn't want to use the motor or rush down the river. He said fine.

I also finally admitted to myself that this "vacation" was not going to be a walk on the beach. I paddled like one possessed for the rest of the day, ignoring the aches and using every bit of brainpower to figure out a more efficient stroke.

Pride and the survival instinct kept me going when my arm and emotions went numb. I realized I couldn't just say, "Well, I've had enough, I think I'll head home now." Barring a major emergency, the only way out was to paddle out – a sobering, but exciting thought.

The excitement – and the rain – continued Tuesday as we traveled to Churchill Dam and awaited our turn at Chase Rapids.

It was the busiest week on the waterway so far this year, so several groups already were unloading before entering the Class III rapids. A ranger trucked everyone's gear beyond the whitewater.

One of Kenn's notes: "This is done because over the years too many travelers have tipped over and lost everything to the bottom."

As we watched other groups leave, it became clearer why Ray had been worried about our lack of skill.

After several days of rain, the river was high, the current fast and the rocks huge, black, and ominous. My thoughts veered from bravado – if other canoeists could do it so could I – to a sick sort of feeling I realized was fear.

We followed Kenn and Ray through the rapids and our first mistake was following them too closely. When trouble slowed them down, we crashed right into them. We disentangled easily enough, but never had time to regroup. My thoughts seemed to be crawling in comparison with the speed of our canoe. Just when I realized what we should be doing – and as the bow person it was my call – it would be too late to do it. Kenn's note, this was my first time in the bow, I was finding this to be true also. Before I could even register what was happening, we spun into the middle of the river and got firmly wedged on two giant rocks. (Note:

it was Ray who kept us from doing the same thing.) Roberta said, "We tried to push off with our paddles, but the river just pushed us back."

Downstream Ray climbed out and began heading up the bank. We debated sitting tight until he arrived, but I hated sitting there, like sitting ducks, waiting for rescue.

So, we got out at either end of the canoe, standing nearly waist deep in the rushing water, and tried to maneuver it off the rocks. At one point the canoe keeled over and half filled with water – we thought we were goners. But eventually we freed it, climbed in, and carefully – like steering a water-filled bathtub – paddled downstream.

It was a triumph of stubborn pride and luck over ignorance and inexperience. The best thing we did was not panic., Ray said. The worst was getting downstream of the canoe.

But we made it, and we were utterly, completely exhilarated. The high lasted long after we bailed the canoe and finished the rapids. And since we'd already messed up pretty badly and survived, the river held fewer terrors.

That was the good part of the day. The lowest point of the whole trip lay just ahead.

I had been wet for most of the day so maybe it's understandable I didn't think to drink any water. Then when we made camp, the first thing I did was the worst thing I could have done. I had a cup of tea. Its diuretic properties drained what fluid I had left. I was badly dehydrated without realizing it.

All night I shivered like someone with an ancient plague. I couldn't get warm even wearing wool hat and jacket in the sleeping bag. I wondered if I'd be able to go on. But the next morning, I finally put two and two together and started drinking water. My improvement was immediate and from then on, I drank religiously.

MOOSE ENDS PERFECT DAY

As if to make up for the horrible night, Wednesday was a perfect day. The sun blazed, the wind stayed down, and we covered miles and miles of Long Lake, with what seemed like no effort. Each day the rattle and clank in my left arm died down more quickly and sometimes I felt I could paddle forever.

All day, George and I meandered along laughing and talking and feeling as if we didn't have a care.

One of the longest running jokes was the extent and nature of our hunger. Not that Ray didn't supply plenty of food, but it was so . . . so wholesome. Beans, rice, spaghetti, muffins, biscuits – even homemade donuts. Actually, quite inventive when you consider it had to last four people a week with no chance to refresh the cooler's ice.

But I dreamed of a medium-rare cheeseburger with fries and the largest glass of milk I could lift, and just one crisp, juicy apple.

We amused ourselves by wondering if a confirmed nature lover like Ray would mind if a Burger King – tastefully designed, of course – were erected nearby with a paddle through. And I kept thinking of those cartoons where shipwrecked companions began to resemble roast

turkeys to one another.

With the sun high and hot, we stopped at Cunliffe Island and hung everything out to dry, so the camp looked like a town after a tornado.

We had our one and only chance to bathe and it took more courage than I expected to walk into that brown river water. The bugs finally drove me under, but the cold water forced me right back to the surface. After a few quick dips, I felt great – but I'm really glad I didn't know until later about the giant bullfrog living in that little cove.

I tried to manage minor cleanups every day, even though a look into the mirror after the first full day was quite discouraging. It revealed a bright red gash across my forehead – I have no idea how I got it – that made me look like one of the Manson followers.

My hair was so plastered down with bug spray and rain that no matter how I combed it I looked exactly like Hitler – if Hitler had lived to be 90.

But Wednesday's sun not only dried our gear, it almost, made us giddy. We joked and talked until nearly dusk, when I left for one last trip to the outhouse, aptly nicknamed the "hole of hell".

I was about ten yards away when I heard a tremendous crashing ahead. I looked up to see a moose about 30 or 40 yards away and running like a racehorse straight at me.

I ran, or more precisely jumped like a jackrabbit to the right of the outhouse, getting in just as the moose went by on the left. I couldn't help giggling as I latched the hook and eye on the door. It seemed pathetically inadequate to stop the huge creature. But I locked it just the same.

Then I stood on the commode and looked through the wire window. The moose, which had a calf with her, stopped about 15 yards away, between me and the camp. "Guys, there's a moose coming," I yelled.

No reply, just a flurry of movement in camp. I hollered again – Ray had warned us terrible things could happen to those who got between a moose and her calf. Finally, my husband yelled back, "We know," in an ironic tone.

Ray called out with concern,

"Roberta, you stay in that outhouse," but I burst out laughing when I yelled back, "Don't worry."

A flash from Kenn's camera got the moose moving, and I moved, too, my legs as shaky as my laughter as I ran back to camp. After that, I always whistled or sang on the way to the outhouse, I still wanted to see wildlife – just not that close.

Kenn's note: The rangers had made a new campsite to help with crowding on busy weeks. It was on a small island, and Ray had wanted to try it out. When we put-in to see moose tracks going through the campsite. We had a movie camera with zoom lens, and we had been practicing with it. When we left the island and rounded a corner there was a moose about to cross from right to my left. I picked up the camera and when I viewed the moose, she looked like she was going to step into the canoe. I said, "Look out, Ray." He said, "Kenn, I'm not on zoom."

BATTLE OF THE BUGS

It's now Thursday, it poured, the bugs were awful, and I was amazingly cheerful in spite of it all.

I never got used to the bugs or the choking taste of the bug spray. Ray told us the black flies would be gone and the mosquitoes much lighter in July or August. Small consolation. In one battle of the bugs, we were completely routed. All four of us were in one canoe, searching for wildlife just before sunset. Kenn paddled hard to get closer to a moose and the canoe bashed into the bushes. A swirling, biting tornado of mosquitoes poured out as if ours was the first red blood available in months. Kenn, intent on the moose, hardly noticed, but the rest of us yelled and put the canoe in reverse as if our lives depended on it.

We scrambled back onto the main channel and revved up the motor, but even then, we couldn't outrun the mosquitoes. I nearly got hysterical laughing at the way they clung to Kenn's hat even at top speed. I retreated into the hood of my raincoat and sneered as they snubbed their noses on its rubber surface.

I have been known to carefully free moths and rescue overturned beetles, but my attitude became, "Get them before they get you." When a flattened bug of unknown origin fell out of my jeans, my only thought was, "Hah! You'll never bite again."

In my loathing, I was only following in the footsteps of travelers through the centuries, who without exception complained about the Allagash's "venomous" insects. But much as I hated the bugs, I loved the river more. Some freezing gray winter day, I plan to warm myself with the memory of sailing down the Allagash, canoes side by side, barely paddling as the current pushed us along. Just lazily talking about everything from our childhoods to our dream trip down the Yukon. Even the rain, which pummeled us five days out of seven, couldn't hide the beauty around us. There was a crystal clarity about some places that was hard to believe even while we were experiencing it. I took my pictures in an attempt to capture it, but I really don't think the translation can be made. The loveliness would just hit you, like a thump in your chest.

Thursday, it was raining so hard we had the river to ourselves. A mist floated among the dark green trees circling Round Pond, reminding me of Brigadoon, the enchanted town that appears in the Scottish Highlands just one day each century. I started singing songs from that musical, believing Ray and Kenn were too far ahead to hear.

But later, they told us nothing could have surprised them more. "That was a first," Ray said emphatically.

"In the rain, people get discouraged. Really there's no singing in the rain."

That was probably how we earned a compliment George and I treasure. Friday morning, when we checked in with the ranger at Michaud Farm, she asked Ray how things were going, with an air of commiseration because of all the rain.

"They're tougher than most." My husband overheard him answer. Felt like we'd earned a Purple Heart.

THE HERON ROOKERY

We watched in dismay as our guide, Ray Reitze, left the main branch of the Allagash and began to pole his canoe up Musquacook Stream.

"Maybe we should just wait for them here," I said doubtfully as Ray and Kenn strained mightily against a current swift with rain.

By the fifth day of our week-long trek down the Allagash, I had grown cautious about expending energy that might be sorely needed later.

But my husband, George Krohne, thought we should follow, and I grumpily agreed, so off we went, paddling furiously, yet moving at a snail's pace.

"Ramming speed," I shouted into the wind. We paddled with difficulty to a little cove where a jut of land slowed the current. Then we made a mad diagonal dash across the stream, with me questioning Ray's sanity in a voice I hoped was load enough for him to hear.

We were slipping past the outlet when one last great burst of effort allowed us to slide into another backwater and slowly paddle on, puffing with relief.

Ray and Kenn waited for us around the corner with big grins. "Congratulations," they said. "You passed the test."

"This better be worth it," I answered. And it was. In the trees ahead was the osprey's nest we'd spotted from afar, but as a bonus there were five herons' nests next door, with a whole flock of the ancient-looking birds posing on various limbs like models for an Egyptian tomb painting.

As we paddled back to the river, though, I thought not about the herons, but about something we and many others before us had been taught on this waterway.

Nothing comes easily on the Allagash. There are great highs and great lows and only the traveler himself knows if one is worth the

Kenn Brooks, left, and Ray Reitze move in for a closer look at an osprey's nest high above Musquacook Stream.

other. And then only at the end.

BACK TO THE REAL WORLD

Thursday and Friday the people pressure on the waterway doubled as groups frantically tried to finish up. There was fierce competition for campsites and a traffic jam of sorts at Allagash Falls.

Several groups portaged while we did and nearly every man, I talked to said wistfully he wished his wife had come, but she was afraid of the bugs, hated canoes, didn't like camping or whatever.

The 40-foot falls impressed me, but the place I liked best was Finley Bogan. The water was still clear, reflecting the leafy maples lining the banks, and everything was so green and fresh you wanted to fill your lungs with air and never let it out.

We probably could have pushed on to the end Friday, but we camped early and finished Saturday morning in bright sunshine. It's an indication of how much my perspective had altered, that 13 miles now seemed a leisurely excursion.

We breezed through Twin Brook Rapids because the water was so high. In fact, high water made the whole trip easier and faster. Ray thought we gained at least an hour a day. But it also spoiled the fishing, so we never used any of the gear we lugged for seven days.

As we approached Allagash Village my stomach turned as sounds of the real world filtered through. No one wanted to admit it when we heard the first car, but the buzz of a lawn mower signaled, the adventure was almost over.

I was filthy, I smelled like 25 layers of bug spray, sweet and stale smoke. I seemed to have more bites than body – even my scalp was bumpy. But I also was very happy. Not only had we made two friends in Ray and

Kenn, but I felt a door had opened to a life filled with many more rivers, campfires, and moose. And I know I wouldn't be afraid to pay the price for finding them.

Of all the paddling songs I sang on the Allagash, the one that kept occurring was a Beatles' tune that starts out "Blackbird singing in the dead of night." I thought I was singing it because of the many red winged blackbirds that ranged over and around us.

But about halfway through the trip I began to wonder if it was another line that kept bringing it to my mind. "All my life, I was only waiting for this moment to arrive."

By Roberta Scruggs

Traveled with – George Krohne

Ray Reitze   Kenn Brooks

Dan Pelley, a guide that was retiring, gave Ray the lead for the firemen from Providence, R.I. They worked so many days on and had time off and then repeated. There were three shifts, days, evenings, and early mornings. The crews usually stayed together and bonded as a group. Those who had worked up to four weeks' vacation time, would take time with family and keep one or two weeks to do something as a group. They had been on many trips all over the place and had been on the Colorado River and thought they might like to do the St. John River Trip.

They made plans to go, but only 11, an odd number signed up to go, and I was to be the 12th one. Ray had to make four canoes to do the trip. He and I got three done and Ray rented a canoe at Pelletier's Campground

owned by Norman L'Italien.
Someone in their group was bringing one 17' tripper made by Old Town Canoes and sold by L.L. Bean.

I was going to be the extra person to make it two men per canoe. I had things packed and was staying overnight with Ray and Nan. I was there when they got the call saying that one of the firemen had broken an ankle on their last fire call before their vacation. That meant I was no longer needed to complete the group, but I decided to stay and help them get packed up for the trip. The next morning when they were due in, Ray and I were making a last check on gear and how it was packed. They arrived and I saw them off and then drove two hours home.

They all drove to Norman L'Italien's and then you all drove to Dicky and left your vehicles there and then Norman took you all into Baker Lake.

When Nancy got the call that Peter's brother had died and was trying to get a message to Ray about getting Peter off the river, it took the warden all day in his efforts to find him. The warden then walked into 7 Islands Campsite with that message. The warden wanted to just take Peter out and Ray said no. Ray had the warden go to Norman's, so Norm could make the swap and get Peter out to St. Francis and get his truck at Dicky Check Point and be on regular roads so he would not get lost. If Peter were to go out, there would be a canoe with only one person in it.

It was Memorial Day weekend and when I got home, I did not unpack the car completely, only my duffle bag of clothes. I came into the house and all I had taken out of it was one set of underwear. In doing that I put my mosquito net on the bed, and it got left behind later.

My Mother and Father-in-law came up on Monday Night to play cards and about 9 pm my sister Nancy called to say they had a problem with the trip. "Do you remember Peter the person in charge of the group of firemen?" I said, "Yes". "Well one of his brothers died and we have to get him off the river to go back home. We would have to bring him out and one of the other firemen would have to give up his trip and bring out a canoe. But I was wondering as you were planning on going, could you be in St. Francis by 5:00 o'clock tomorrow night, so Norman could take you in and bring him out?"

"I'll be in your living room in two hours or about midnight, have the couch ready." Then I told Nila and her folks what was going on, grabbed my bag of clothes and left without the net which was on the bed.

When I got to Nancy's, I quietly let myself in and found a note on the table saying April had to be up early and go to college in Waterville. I left a note for April, my niece, to wake me up and we could have breakfast together. We did, then we left about 6:30 am.

Nancy had let Norman know I was coming.

I drove to Newport and got on I-95 North. Who did I see going by the Newport Exit, just my classmate Steve Wood driving the Wood's Mill Company Tractor-trailer loaded with wooden shipping pallets headed "Down-East". I know he had a governor on the truck and a radar detector, a very safe bet to follow until I exited for Route #11 in Sherman and north to Patten, and on up the road.

Now I had been from north to south four times on trips on the Allagash that ended in Allagash Village. Now it was time to reverse the direction. I knew I would follow it to my destination, but could I make it by 5:00 pm?

I had gone quite a few miles to Grindstone Village when I came to a small store. Their driveway in front had been taken away by road widening, the parking was across the street by the railroad tracks. A road from the East came out there, if they wished to cross and go West, they first had to cross the tracks and go West on the other side of them. Making it a dangerous intersection.

I went into the store for snacks and soda, and as I was coming out, I heard this tractor-trailer truck coming, using Jake-Brakes to slow himself down, to go through the bad intersection that I just described. I stood on the deck and watched him go by, the minute he got across the tracks and by the intersection he started shifting gears and picking up speed as he went by the toothpick factory. I said to myself, he knows the road. I think I want to follow that guy as he knows when to go down a hill fast with no problems at the bottom and having enough speed to go up the next hill or he is slowing up going down because there is a problem to look out for. We had just come down one and around a gentle curve when we met a "Statie" coming. He was going pretty fast, but with no blue lights on, he points at the truck driver and then me as if to say slow down but kept on going, you know to an important meeting. Ha! Ha!

I followed the truck all the way up to Eagle Lake until he turned into Fort Kent High School. This worked and I made St. Francis about 4:45 pm. Norman L'Italien was my contact person and the warden had not contacted him yet. He had me park out back of the little store at his campground in case I had to sleep in it for the night. An hour later he said the warden had called to say it had taken all day to contact Ray on the waterway. He had walked into 7 Island Campsite to find Ray. It had rained the night before and all the next day, so Ray and crew had set tight. Ray and the warden made plans for Norman to bring me in and take Peter out. Norman asked the warden to take me in, as he had something else he had to do. Norman took me home for supper and then back to my car where I curled up in the back seat for an uncomfortable night.

The warden was there real early the next morning and we left for Priestly Bridge to meet Ray and the crew and bring Peter out to Norman's and then up to his truck. Riding in his pickup I felt like a trainee, and I was asking all kinds of questions about the job and the area. When we got to the bridge-site we found it had been washed out by the spring flood waters. It was under construction and as we sat there and waited, two moose came out of the woods on the other side and walked over and inspected the excavator, then they crossed the road and went by a bulldozer before disappearing into the woods.

When Ray and his travelers arrived, that's when I found out that it had rained so hard the one day that they stayed in camp all day, which was why the warden had a hard time finding him at 7 Islands.

Campsites we stayed at:

Baker Lake

1. Southwest Brook
2. Burntland Brook went under Nine Mile Bridge
3. Seven Islands two nights

Priestley Bridge was washed out and under repair; this was our meeting place.

Priestley Rapids went through

4. Simmons Farm Campsite

   Basford Rips went through

   Big Black Rips went through

   Big Black River went by

5. Big Black Campsite went for a
   walk.

   Ferry Crossing Campsite went by

   Seminary Brook went by

   Long Rapids went through 6.

   Castonia Rapids went through

   Schoolhouse Rips went through

   Fox Brook Rapids went through 7.

   Poplar Island Rapids went through

   Dicky Check Point went by

   Big Rapids Class #3 upset tip over

   St. Clair Island went by

   Dicky take out

My first night at Simmons Farm
Campsite, after Priestly Bridge, I
know they brought a lot of food,
something special for every supper

meal, because of their numbers they wanted to help out with food and the two cooks wanted to cook. My first meal was fish. They sure knew how to feed a crew!

Two girls came in late and set up a tent behind ours. They told us they had been dropped off at Baker Lake and because of low water. They had a very hard time lining the canoe and walking for miles, then the rain brought up the water level.

The girls were up, and on the water first, only because there was so many of us.

On my second day when we got to the Big Black campsite, we got wood quick and built a fire under a spicket made of a "Stainless Steel Rod" on legs. The rod was pushed down the leg bone and out the other end. They had forgotten the handle and all they had to turn it with was a pair of vise grips. After setting up tents we all took turns turning and rolling the leg of beef while it cooked. What a meal it made for being miles out in the woods and miles downriver.

After supper Ray and I and a few others walked the high bank on the left to overlook the next set of rapids. Two girls came down river moved to the right across from us and one of them stood up. Ray said, "She is reading the water ahead and picking her path down through for her group of canoes that were following her." Then they ran the rapids and camped down river and finished ahead of us.

At one place on the right there was the top of a fir tree, up high in a stand of spruce trees. That had been hit by ice which propelled it high up into the trees, taking all the limbs and bark off as it did so. It looked like a large spear thrown at a bird upon a tree higher than a man could reach.

I enjoyed talking with my canoe mate as his folks had immigrated from Hungary. He and I followed in the middle of the group. In talking with them, most of them said they would do it again, or maybe the Allagash. A few said they had a good time but would not do it again as once was enough.

My third day out, we followed the girls' example and ran the rapids. As we came to the Castonia Farm Campsite, we found that the flood waters had cut the left bank back on the corner exposing a huge rock as big as two cars setting on top of each other, that had never before been seen.

This trip was after ice out and spring rains. The water was still very cold, and two days of rain had brought the water back up. We were at Big Rapids and some of us were already ashore to look at the washed-out area, as the last canoe (the rented one, an Old Town 17' Tripper) turned to come into shore, they turned it over. They had a cooler with a bad cover with the condiments: butter, relish, mustard, catchup, etc., all went to the bottom, leaving the styro-foam cooler to float away.

Ray and I were standing nearest the canoes talking; we had not taken off our life jackets. We went out after one of them, as did two others. One was on the downstream side and the other guy was holding onto the upstream side of the turned-over canoe. Ray did not want them trying to get into our canoe and turning us over. Ray told me and them not to do any thinking; he would have to hit someone with a pole if they did not follow his advice. Ray took the setting pole, cut a diagonal and let the upstream canoe float to us. He then got the downstream guy over the side of our canoe and got him to shore. The other canoe circled to the up-side and got the other guy. I can still see the expressions of the cold getting to them. Ray had them hang onto the side of the canoes, one to each. As we paddled them ashore, their canoe went down river. Some of the others started a fire, and the wet ones took off their clothes and got into dry ones. They huddled by the fire to get warm. I was so tired from paddling that Ray had me help with the fire, as he and the others went to pick up their floating gear and the canoe which had fetched up in the shallows just below the rapids.

We always travel with clothes and gear in air-tight bags that float.

After getting them warmed up we went to Dicky and took out the canoes, loaded up and went out. When we came off the water Ray and I rode down to Pelletier's Campground to return the canoe and get my car. The firemen went down

Route #11 and kept on going down the pike (I-95) Rhode Island bound.

I went to Ray's to help unload and put things away, ate, and went home.

LAKE PLACID TRIP: STOVE BLOWING UP

Ray decided to make a trip to Lake Placid, N.Y. in the Adirondack Mountains to see if he could find a sporting goods outfitter to sell one of his Cedar Strip Canoes or maybe get some orders.

Ray asked me if I would like to go and keep him company. We immediately made plans to take Route #2 all the way out and back. What a beautiful trip, all the little villages, farms, lakes, and views galore. The site of the ski jumps, all kinds of places had practice jumps. Lots of helpful people.

We had a canoe on boat racks on Ray's Bronco and did not turn any interest. Seemed to me that they were more into brook fishing gear. We found a place to get off the road and slept in the truck.

That second morning we got up, yep, the canoe was still on top. Ray lowered the tailgate to set up the Coleman stove to cook breakfast. At some point in our travels a cigarette lighter had fallen into the bottom of the stove and slid under the burner undetected. Ray started it up, put a pan on it, and in seconds when it blew up, I was off, I mean like a shot out of a cannon, running down the road.

Ray hollered at me, "Kenn, come on back. You aren't dead."

Nancy has told me that Ray has told this story over and over again, laughing all the time. This must have struck his funny bone to be so vividly remembered over and over again.

It was a short trip. Ray decided that we weren't going to sell the canoe there, so we headed home. It was still a nice trip, for we saw things coming back we missed on the way out, as you always do. I always have fun with Ray, his philosophy on life is so sound.

Thanks, brother Ray for everything. Kenn

ALLAGASH WILDERNESS WATERWAY TRIP WITH MY SON RICHARD

In planning this trip with Ray, it was decided that Rich and I would do the upper part alone and then meet up with him and finish as a group. Ray had a week trip planned with friends, also taking two college girls to teach them how to pole in shallow water.

Poling: By standing up, so you can see the channel better, using the pole for balance as well as a method to push your canoe forward and around rocks if need be. The girls were going on other trips with college programs later in the summer and wanted to be able to do the poling.

Ray's group was going to put in at Long Lake Check Point where the Realty Road crosses the thoroughfare between Umsaskis Lake and Long Lake. Rich and I were to go by and camp at "Sam's Campsite" the designated meeting place. I had been trying for two years to schedule this trip with Rich and Ray.

After going over Ray's list of things to take: sleeping bag for 20-degrees, air

mattress, rain gear, jacket, hat w/brim, sunglasses, suntan lotion (SPF 15), bathing suit, towel, washcloth (two complete changes of clothing including long pants and shirt), sweater or sweat shirt, (sneakers, boots or shoes with tread), personal toilet articles, favorite paddle if they have one (optional), a dry bag, insect repellent, camera and film, 1 cup with a handle for hot and cold drinks, fishing gear and license, (if you wear glasses – bring safety straps) and medicine if needed.

I made racks for Richard's truck. After the last trip with Ray, I found I needed a new tent. At L.L. Bean's I purchased a four-man tent and a second "Dry Bag" for our clothes. By meeting Ray in the middle of our trip, we did not need to carry two weeks of food.

We packed up and left Standish on a Saturday morning. On our way we made a stop to see my friends David and Carol Amerin in Abbott Village at their Real Estate office. Missed them and left my business card.

We were in Greenville for gas, ice, milk, and snacks between one and two o'clock. Down the hill, turn right before you run into Moosehead Lake's lower bay, now all dirt roads. Lily Bay Road to Telos Road, a short way – No Way! It's ten miles on Lily Bay Road going by Lily Bay State Park. About seven miles to Kokadjo on the west end of First Roach Pond. We continued northeast on Silas Hill Road fifteen miles to Ragged Lake, four miles to the southeast end of Caribou Lake and turned right onto Golden Road. Six miles to Ripogenus Lake, 1/2-mile to Ripogenus Dam (a beautiful sight), another ½-mile to Ripogenus Gorge, and another ½mile to the Telos Road on the left (not well marked when we went through) 43 ½-miles from Greenville and it's getting late.

Then in some six miles you go around the north end of Harrington Lake, and six or seven miles to Telos Check Point. At this point the road is gated and tended by employees of the North Maine Woods. You have to check in to let them know your planned route and exit point, and then pay a daily fee for the use of the roads.

They could not give us a good estimate as to the distance to the road into Indian Pond. You have to go around the Arm of Chamberland Lake. Well, we later found out it was six miles to the Chamberland Bridge still on the Telos Road, four miles along the bottom of the boot, at the toe of the boot make a sharp left turn and another five miles to the road we wanted. The road signs are not very good in the North Maine Woods. I wanted to make Thoreau's Camp Site on Pillsbury Island before dark. This island was named after the writer Henry David Thoreau who camped there on one of his trips.

It was getting later, almost dusk. Rich was hurrying, and the turn was at the top of a little rise, and he was right on top of it. He cut in, bang, a flat tire cut on the rocky shale. As we were getting the tire off, two Park Rangers came along and stopped to see if they could help, but we had the spare already put on.

Five miles to a gate and a small stream, the place where we went to leave the truck. The stream runs from Indian Pond to Eagle Lake about a quarter mile in.

The Rangers had gone through the gate on their way to Lock Dam Campsite. Richard had gotten a phone call just before we left home that his father-in-law in Florida had been admitted to a hospital for having a Heart Attack. Rich wanted to talk to the Rangers on their way out, so they would know our trip plans if they had to get a message to us.

We got the canoe off the truck racks and took it to the brook. We could see that the water was very high. Next, we moved our gear down to the water's edge, parked the truck and hid the key for Norman L'Italien and his crew who would be moving it to Allagash Village.

Still, no Rangers as we packed everything into the canoe. Reluctant to leave, we went back to the gate. We could now see them at the bottom of the hill doing something at the back of their truck; then one of them got up into the pickup body and backed out. It was getting later still, so Rich decided to run down to talk to them. They were fixing a flat tire.

When he got back, we started off. This was my third trip at this point. The first time the water was very low. We could put all we could into the backpacks. We put the rest in the canoe and then walked to the lake. Ray had told us that at some time in the past there had been an old logging campsite there, and that there was a lot of broken glass in the water. The second time we were able to put all the gear into the canoe, walk it a short way before getting in to paddle to the lake. This time we could paddle right away. When we had advanced to where we could see Eagle Lake, it became evident that beavers had constructed a very large dam backing up the flow of water. It took most of an hour to find a safe spot, set all the gear over, struggle to get the canoe over and reload it.

We did not know it was a little over a mile to the campsite as we went by Bear Mountain Point, till we crossed a large cove. We could hardly see up the gut between the mainland and Pillsbury Island, which loomed up on the right.

We could not seem to find the campsite. Was it my memory? I thought we should have been there.

I said to Rich, "We must set up the tent right now, right spot or not." As we put ashore there was a small area where we found a cleared spot with flashlights and the tent went up fairly quickly. We made a fire and warmed up a can of Dinsmore Soup, ate, and went to bed.

The next morning, I was up first for a pee run. I saw another path and followed it a short way which took me to the main campsite; we had made it! After a breakfast of cereal and milk, (we had milk for three days before the end of the ice.), we packed up and as we were leaving to find the "Tramway" to see the Railroad Trains, we looked back to the sign for "Thoreau's Campsite".

The first time I was here with Ray they had a white post in the water near shore as a guide to the entrance to the tramway site for the post sets back in the woods out of sight. It was gone. Someone has to tell you where to look for it, and I had started looking for it too soon. We would not have seen the large Bear Tracks on the sand bar where we put in to investigate. So, we decided to take off our boots and walk a ways in the warm shallow water. When we got closer, we began to see railroad rails and other metal parts in the water. We found the channel made from the deep water to shore. We went back and brought the canoe up.

When the Northwoods Wilderness Waterway was created, they wanted to return it to nature. They wanted people to stay at designated campsites, so signs naming them were allowed. All other guidepost, arrows, and signs were taken down.

Years before the State had built a train shed over the two Railroad Locomotives to protect them. Now they had burnt the shed down around the trains.

I think Rich was quite impressed to see the two Railroad Engines setting side by side. One weighs 90 ton; the other 100 ton and they are starting to list to one side. If nothing is done, they will be found on their sides. (I have since heard that some group has worked on them to prevent this from happening.)

You can also walk along two old tracks and see the remains of the log hauling cars. I didn't count them but, I'm guessing there are between 50 & 80 of them in disrepair with the platform bodies dropped down over the axles. At one of the old building foundations, we found a tree growing up through a piece of copper stovepipe roof flashing. The tree was already exceeding the hole in the center of it.

I set a bottle of Mt. Dew on a walkway along the engine boiler, as we walked back and took photos of the trains. One of the photos shows the Mt. Dew bottle. We spent a couple of hours exploring before we left.

When we were halfway across Eagle Lake, I wanted a drink; it was then that I remembered where I left it. I had to dig out another one as we paddled by Hog Island (where the loggers kept pigs without fences) then by Farm Island. Now the wind came up as we passed Priestly Point. We were looking for the next campsite called the Pumphandle; we could not see the sign. As the wind began blowing like hell, it and the waves kept taking us out. We turned left and went straight in and tried going along shore about forty feet out. With the wind and waves still worse, we put ashore and lined the canoe along shore and found the sign hidden in alder bushes. Yep, we had found the right place, but we still had to get around a bunch of large rocks. Richard went wading to line the canoe and get us to the sandy boat landing.

(Lining means holding onto ropes at the bow and stern of the canoe and walking the canoe through shallow water like a large dog on a leash.)

We looked around, found a good level spot, and set up the tent with the wind still finding its way through the trees. We rounded up firewood and then cut the alder bushes to expose the sign for a better view from out on the lake. We pulled the alders near the fire pit to put on the fire later, for a smudge against blackflies and just to get rid of the evidence.

On the back side of this peninsula are two high bluffs looking West, called First and Second Ridge. With two hours of daylight left, we decided to hike up. The Rangers keep a good trail up to the first ridge. But wouldn't you know there had been a recent wind blow and there were a lot of trees down in the trail at the bottom where it crosses a wet area. We worked our way up when we got there, we found that you can enjoy the view in both directions for a longways, from whence you came and to where you were going to advance. We were hoping to see part of the sunset before heading back down, but we had been there only a little while when we heard a motor. Only Rangers may use motorboats to get around, everyone else has to paddle.

We could see him going over to Pillsbury Island in the distance. Was he looking for us with a message for Richard? Or was he only on his nightly rounds? So, we started down and heard him go over the tramway then back by Farm Island to our campsite as we were descending. We hurried a little faster; sure enough he was waiting for us at the campsite. He had no message for Rich.

He said, "Cut a few bushes, I see." "Ya," I said. "We could not see the sign from out on the lake." "Ya, I know," he said. "That was on my list of things to get done."

"Well," I said. "May I ask you two questions? How many people put in down at Churchill Dam and come up the lake this way to here? How many people put in at Indian Pond or come across the isthmus from Chamberland Lake through the tramway?"

He said, "97% of them come the way you did." Then, I told him about the trip from Indian Pond, the beaver dam and not being able to see the sign for Thoreau's campsite or even knowing you had reached Pillsbury Island. You don't see the sign until you're on your way out and only when you look back.

"Well, good point. I'll take care of it next time I'm over there," he said.

He was very nice about it. I thought he probably could have given us holy hell or written us up.

After he left, we started a fire, ate while feeding alders to the fire and talking about the day's adventure and then we went to bed. As they say, "Life by the yard is awfully hard, but inch by inch it's a cinch." The end of day two.

The morning of day three we met the Ranger coming from the Zeigler Campsite as we went by crossing Eagle Lake's Lower Bay. Just after passing the Little Eagle Campsite, the breeze came up again. By the time we reached a very large rock with a flat top, the size of a house roof, a couple of feet out of the water making a good landing spot, we put in on it. The wind was making whitecaps coming across Round Pond right at us. (You could have put a dozen canoes on that rock. I was impressed by the size of the rock as the water was now exposing the rock that was usually under water.)

We waited two hours, the wind no better, no worse. I said to Rich, "This is not any worse than yesterday." After looking at the map, I decided the best route would be staying on the left side near and into shore, wanting to land if we had trouble, even if it was a lot longer. Another two and ½-hours going into the wind we made it to John's Bridge on the Cyr Road crossing and stopped for lunch. The morning hadn't produced any wildlife. After looking at the map again we decided to stay left again going down Churchill Lake. By late afternoon, we made Schofield Point Campsite on the upstream side of the point. After we set up camp. We walked back up the shoreline and found the spring for good water. (Which Ray had showed me on a previous trip.)

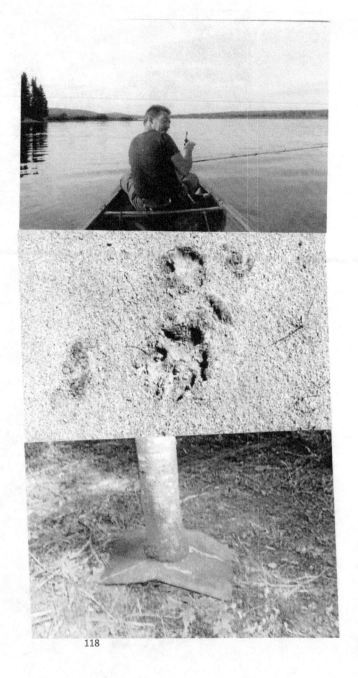

Day four we went down the rest of Churchill Lake. No wind today, a beautiful day, we stayed left again around Schofield Point. I was wondering if lefty Richard was having something to do with it. It was still a longways down the lake to Chamberland Dam. We still had to go by "High Point Campsite" on the left and the "Jaws Campsite" on the right. After going by High Bank, two guys went by us in kayaks just burning up calories into Heron Lake, more of a small pond at the head of Churchill Dam. We could see all the way across. The kayakers were almost there and the Rangers on the dock. They could see us and held the equipment truck, as they knew we were the last voyagers expected for the day. We unloaded and put our stuff into the truck to be moved down beyond the white water, as Chase Rapids are rated Class III.

As we waited our turn at the fast water, I showed Rich around

Churchill Depot. The large building still stands that was a dining hall downstairs and a dance hall upstairs, way back in the day. On the other side of the Dam stands a very large barn; you access it by the road built on top of the Dam. The Rangers have made it into an exhibit of things left from the logging days.

There is a very large wood-splitter on the outside, a sight to see. One side goes up while the other side comes down striking the piece of wood just placed there; as it starts another cycle the pieces have to be moved out of the way, and another piece off the nearby pile sets up again. In my mind I could paint a picture of two crews of 4 to 6 men on each side doing this in alternating cycles.

We had decided to have lunch after the big run. I can't say I took the same path as Ray did on the other trip. Did we hit any rocks? Yes, I can't deny it as the white scraps on the bottom of the canoe are proof of it. Rich broke a paddle on one of the big ones, but we made the seven miles without hanging up on any of them and not getting wet.

Rich did say upon reaching the old bridge site, "I'm glad that you were in the stern."

The Kayakers and two other groups were having lunch, having made the same decision to eat after the rapids. The kayakers left first, as they told us they were trying to make the ten-day trip in five days and were on schedule. The other two groups left thirty minutes apart to keep from jamming up on the water, so each could enjoy the trip, although. Their time was limited more than us, they were trying to go down to the end of Umsaskis Lake and make camp. We lagged behind knowing that we were OK, making good time. When we came to the Meadows Campsite, one of the groups had changed their minds and was setting up camp there.

We went to the Chisholm Brook Campsite which sets on a high bluff looking out over Umsaskis Lake. We tied off the canoe and toted everything up. After a short rest break, we looked the place over and chose a level spot with a view back upstream, as I thought the wind off the big lake would be a possible problem. After we set up the tent and ate supper we looked down and saw our first moose in the swamp below our vantage point. She crossed the river in the direction of The Meadows Campsite. Did they see her I wondered.

We stayed up until dark, then off to bed only to be awakened in the middle of the night. The wind had come up and was whipping at us from upriver, so much for my thinking. The wind grabbed the tarp we had put over the picknick table.

It was flapping like a flag, as the lines on the near side had been torn loose, the other side was just barely holding.

Like firemen we jumped into our pants, and we tried to beat the wind, but the wind won as it deposited the tarp into the trees. Had it not been for that line of trees and brush on the other side of the bluff, the tarp would have sailed out onto Umsaskis Lake. We rolled it up and put it in the tent, then went around checking all the tent tie downs while tying one corner to a nearby birch tree. The rest of the night passed uneventfully.

Day five came up with a beautiful sunrise. Over eggs and bacon, we studied the map again. I felt relieved of my fear of being late to meet up with Ray on time. I should have taken more faith in what Ray had said, "You can make it easily," as he knew we had time, as long as we had no major catastrophe.

Picking up and packing everything down the hill and loading the canoe, it took a little longer; we saw the other party head out ahead of us, never to be seen again. Umsaskis Lake took the rest of the morning. Again, we hugged the left side of center as there was a big cove on the right side.

We next came to Sandy Point Campsite at the edge of Long Lake and the Ranger Station Check Point. We knew that was the end of Ray's auto ride in and where we would meet him, so we stopped for a pit stop, lunch and good look around.

Then we went under the American Realty Road Bridge and down the thoroughfare in shallow water to Long Lake. There always seems to be a reason to stay left. This time Sam's Campsite, the appointed meeting place, was on that side. It was about twelvish when we set up the tent and camp. Next, we gathered up firewood enough for two nights. (Richard and Rich are the same person.)

Richard had been wanting to go fishing, so I paddled him around in a much lighter canoe, as it was empty now. We went down to where Chemquasaboomticook Stream empties in. He caught three small fish and released them.

Back to camp for beans and hot dogs the canned kind. As we were putting ashore, we could see the big black cloud coming and then pure white ones started pushing their way over it, billowing up real high over it. The whole formation was only about three hundred yards wide and moving very fast. We stood there watching them. I got my camera and got photos of them, expecting rain at any moment, but it passed over. It was something to see the contrast of colors. It was very evident that someone, somewhere to the southeast was going to get wet. Before dusk we went looking for moose, no luck.

Day six, this was our morning to sleep in and we did a little bit, but in early to bed – getting up early got us. So, again we took the lighter canoe fishing, but Rich was not having any luck in the river. We then decided to head up Chemquasaboomticook Stream. We had gone only a short way when a mother and calf stood on the sand bank on our right. The moose crossed to another sand bank and followed a very tiny stream out of sight.

The fishing was no better, so we decided to just go exploring. About a mile and a half up, there was a sporting camp on a high bank on the right. The stream was getting narrower and shallower and about three turns later it was as far as we could go; we were hitting bottom.

When we came back to the dock at the camp the friendly owner came down to chat with us. He said, "I don't usually get visitors by water." He went on to tell us the summer had been so hot that the fish had returned to the deep water in the river.

He then invited us for a tour of his establishment. He had photos of the area long ago; I can't remember all the history stories.

On the way back out an eagle perched in a tree watching our progress. When we went under his tree, not having seen him, his departure startled us, but what a beautiful flight path as he glided out of sight. Back at camp for lunch, rather than just sit and wait for them, we paddled back up to the check point.

As we approached the bridge, we
could hear the logging truck coming
and luckily got to within sight of the

bridge in time to see him fly by in a cloud of dust. How the bridges can withstand all that weight, being hit all of a sudden and the truck be gone just as quick, it's amazing and hard to believe. When they approach, "get the hell out of their way or else."

We looked around and saw no Ranger home as we scouted the area with nice, mowed lawn, and well-kept building. We walked the road quite aways in each direction while waiting.

Ray and crew had traveled from Canaan to St. Francis to meet up with Norman L'Italien. Norm runs a campground and a shuttle service moving vehicles and or people around.

They had traveled from St. Francis to Allagash Village. Then picked up the dirt logging roads to Michaud Farms and went to Priestly Bridge on the St. John River; next, they passed Cunliffe Lake and Clayton Lake on the

American Realty Road. This took them to Long Lake Check Point near Sandy Point each leg (stretch) covering many miles.

Not noon, but two'ish in rolls Norman in his 12-man passenger Sports Van with a trailer in tow. They all got out like sardines from a can, unloaded everything, four canoes, tents and gear, so Norm could leave for home.

The passengers were Raymond and Nancy Reitze, Bennitt Verbeck and Jan Ries his girlfriend, a guide in training with Ray. John Haney and his wife Brenda Gould, Katie Webb and Kenya Perry, two college students.

Next, they put canoes in the water and loaded them up, moved down to Sam's where Rich and I were all set up and reserving the campsite. They

MILLINOCKET

Driver killed in collision with logging truck

A driver was killed Monday when a pickup truck crashed into a logging truck on the Golden Road, a 96-mile private logging road, law enforcement authorities said.

The pickup driver didn't see the logging truck because dust on the road restricted visibility, officials told WABI-TV.

Authorities didn't immediately release the victim's name.

The accident happened on the road west of Baxter State Park in Piscataquis County.

set up tents, and then we all had a good visit close around the table as Ray and Jen started preparing for supper. Rich and I started talking with the students, as they and Rich were the newbies to the rest of us on the trip.

The rest of us had met on previous trips, but it had been a while and updating was in order. Of course, they wanted to know all about our trip so far. Well, I said, "Ray, I know you said I had plenty of time to get here, but I still worried about being late, not dreaming of being a day early. It was a good feeling when we got here." Then, not in complete sentences, I told them what you just read.

In the morning we left for Long Lake Dam knowing spikes in the planks on the bottom of the river were gone and did not need to worry about hitting them with the canoes.

Ya, it's a long lake, a little over halfway down you go by Lost Popple Campsite before reaching Long Lake Dam at a short fast water and dropping down to Cunliffe Island where we stayed the second night with Ray.

More visiting as we set up camp and Jen and Bennett started supper. Ray and I got wood and water. Then Rich and I set up our tent. When we

came over to eat, they were talking about the name they gave my large 4-man tent. "The Taj Mahal." No one would admit it, and the rest would not disclose who was the one to coin the phrase.

The girls were up next; everyone wanted to know an update on them, schools, college and their upcoming canoe trip. When we ran out of "light" we tarried awhile before the fire began to lose its light, turning in for the night.

Next morning up early, had breakfast and left early. We went by Sweeny Campsite with people eating their breakfast. Next was Round Pond, longer than round with its five campsites, we stopped at the last one for lunch. Then Ray took time to teach the girls to pole.

Down a crooked stretch to Marquacook Deadwater. This was where Richard and I went ahead and missed the channel going right into shallow water. We had to cross two sand bars to be able to follow Ray to the left down a very narrow channel, then by Five Finger Brook and Five Fingers Campsite.

At Cunliffe Depot Campsite we walked in to see the old Lombard left in a field which is now all woods.

At Michaud Farms Check Point Ray checked us in. Then it's 2 miles of Finley's Bogan the last big body of water on the way to Allagash Falls.

The water was so clear, reflecting the
leafy maples lining the banks.

Everything was so green and fresh you wanted to fill your lungs with air and never let it out.

We stopped at an old homestead on a high bank on the right. They had been the last couple to live in the area, years after everyone else had gone. Blackberries and raspberries were growing near the old building. Nancy found a fresh pile of bear shit, which it had deposited just before we sent him back into the woods.

Ray told us the story of the people who lived there until their health put an end to it.

Allagash Falls has a forty-foot drop to it. The signs tell you to stay right and take out for the half-mile portage. There are three campsites about halfway across and are usually taken. It's an easy half-day trip to Allagash Village and it's about a half-day portage.

Ray, Richard, and Bennett carried the canoes. With my bad knee I slowly made two trips with backpacks and paddles and the ladies carried gear too. Then we had lunch before going to look at the two faces that can be seen in the rocks with a short walk. Then we moved down to Big Brook Campsite on the right and set up camp followed by supper and a good night sleep after the work of the portage.

The next morning, a half-day out, we loaded up the canoes for the last time, went by Mt. Gargien Rocks, Twin Brook Rapids, Three Mile, and Casey Rapids, a small one as we approached Allagash Village where we heard the first car, no one wanted to admit it signaling the end of the water part of the trip.

We went and got the vehicles and brought them across the street to load them up. Then we went to lunch at the restaurant for a reprieve of days of our own cooking before heading home.

We then went to Ray Porter's in Patten. He made paddles for years. When he sold the paddle business, he started making Pack Baskets up to 2020 two years before he died.

When we left there, Ray got ahead in traffic and stopped for ice cream. We did not see him when we went by to get onto I-95 and headed for their house. We wondered why we could not catch up with him. He said later he just thought we wanted to get on home.

LETTER TO RICHARD AFTER THE CANOE TRIP

I, the undersigned, being of sound mind and body, and in possession of all my faculties, do hereby bequeath to my son, Richard, the following legacy: it is a weird legacy perhaps, Rich, for it consists at this time of no worldly goods whatever except for two paddles and an eighteen-foot canoe.

It seems to me now that this legacy is nothing but an accumulation of memories. Moreover, I am acutely aware that these memories are mine, and therefore – to you – perhaps no legacy at all.

It is hard to define that Allagash trip, but it is so much fun to cherish it. All the planning, making the time, the getting there, the flat tire, the beaver dam, getting over it, through the narrows, finding Thoreau's Campsite in the dark, setting up the tent and fixing supper of Dinsmore Soup.

Rich, you said, "You know it's dark and I'm not scared of the dark anymore." I said, "No, it's kind, it's merciful. It's the end of the day, a good experience and part of life."

We rejoiced in the morning when we saw the lake shining through the alders. The canoe was built to glide on the water with plenty of space for the tent, grub for a week, cooking utensils, Mountain Dew, oh, and your fishing pole.

Then we found the bear tracks in the sand, as big as our hand, where we walked up the beach. We found the abandoned railroad trains, left in those woods, the tree growing up through the copper stovepipe roof vent, when we cut the bushes that almost covered the signs for the campsites.

"Dad how far are we from anyone else?" you said. "Maybe ten miles." I said.

I'll never forget your eyes, eager, happy, wild, elated. Then the wind came up and stranded us on that large rock at the head of the lake. You glanced up once to see ducks fly over, and later you saw the deer swimming, and climb out of the lake and shake off before disappearing into the woods.

This strange thing happened this moment so important in the legacy of remembering. It astonished me, and it still does. You said, "Doggonit, I am awfully happy." After a second, I said, "Why?" "I don't know." "Neither do I." I said, "But I know what you mean."

Do I know? What did you mean? I wish I could say it, and I am afraid to try, but I will. "We'll think of this trip for a long time, Rich."

And that's what I'm doing right now, remembering some 10 years ago. I'm also thinking about the extra day we spent exploring up the brook, while waiting to meet Ray the next day. After finding the hunting lodge, the tour the owner gave us, and the Eagle coming out of the tree for a flyover on our way out.

I can feel the canoe jolt as we touched shore, and you stepped ashore, and we could hear the waves "slap – slap" on it as we pulled it from the water and beached it. For a long time, we heard the first rain drops hit the tarp over the tent and there is no sound I know which can match it.

Now as I put this ill-defined legacy on paper, I can hear the spring rain on the roof. As these things are indescribably good because you and I first shared them on that trip. But still

 it seems strange what a legacy leaves, nothing but a few memories to the legatee. Of all the hunting with you, this trip was the best.

Dad

POSTSCRIPT

 Kenn brooks presents wonderful real-life stories about his experiences navigating the rivers of Northern Maine, cumulatively referred to as

The Allagash. Hope you enjoyed the adventures along with Kenn and his Friends as they witnessed the true nature of the Northern Maine woods and waterways.

As seen during the many trips with his expert Maine Guide Ray Reitze, Jr., the travels are not for those who seek a leisurely day on the waterways. The trek is often hazardous in that canoeists must contend with swirling rapids, hidden obstructions below the waterline, and the unpredictable weather. An occasional unexpected moose in camp at night is always a memorable experience as well.

Readers take part in these real-to-life journeys as they depict the challenges to those willing to accept them. Enjoy the Moment!

TIMOTHY J. OLEARY, III

KENN BROOKS

Made in the USA
Middletown, DE
30 October 2023

41519657R00086

Made in the USA
Middletown, DE
13 June 2023

32534986R00111